THE PROPHECY OF THE
WHITE RIDER

THE PROPHECY OF THE WHITE RIDER

WHITE RIDER

HIS NECESSARY TALENTS WILL BE SUMMONED

C. L. Thomas

iUniverse, Inc.
Bloomington

The Prophecy of the White Rider
His Necessary Talents Will Be Summoned

All quotes, unless otherwise noted, Scriptures are taken from The Holy Bible, King James Version. Copyright © 1972 by Thomas Nelson Inc., Camden, New Jersey 08103.

iUniverse books may be ordered through booksellers or by contacting:

iUniverse
1663 Liberty Drive
Bloomington, IN 47403
www.iuniverse.com
1-800-Authors (1-800-288-4677)

Because of the dynamic nature of the Internet, any web addresses or links contained in this book may have changed since publication and may no longer be valid. The views expressed in this work are solely those of the author and do not necessarily reflect the views of the publisher, and the publisher hereby disclaims any responsibility for them.

Any people depicted in stock imagery provided by Thinkstock are models, and such images are being used for illustrative purposes only.
Certain stock imagery © Thinkstock.

ISBN: 978-1-4620-5071-0 (sc)
ISBN: 978-1-4620-5072-7 (ebk)

Printed in the United States of America

iUniverse rev. date: 09/21/2011

Contents

Narration ix

Chapter 1   The Days Were Dark 1

Chapter 2   The Wind of Destruction 5

Chapter 3   The Lake of the Gallows 8

Chapter 4   The Four Corners of the Earth 12

Chapter 5   Storming the Enemy's Camp 15

Chapter 6   The Lord Promised 19

Chapter 7   The Saluted Swords of Heaven 22

Chapter 8   The Battle of Souls 26

Chapter 9   The Great Army of the Lord 31

Chapter 10   At One With the White Rider 35

Chapter 11   Freedom to the Captives 39

Chapter 12   Victory is as Sweet as Honey 42

Chapter 13   The Favor of Your Love 44

Chapter 14   Teach Them to Ride 46

Chapter 15   The Rider's Song 50

Chapter 16   Commencement 54

Chapter 17   Around the Tabernacle Table 57

Chapter 18   A God of Beginnings and Not Ends 63

Chapter 19   The Sun Rose Fierce 69

Chapter 20 The Sealed Scroll 72

Chapter 21 Pale Mercy 76

Chapter 22 Love Would Be Nurtured and Live 81

Chapter 23 The Hope of the Nations 84

Chapter 24 To Touch the Hearts of Mankind 88

Chapter 25 His Own Purposes 90

Chapter 26 A Message to the Seekers of Love 98

Chapter 27 The Conqueror Rides 101

Summary   A Throne Room Prophecy 103

About the Author 105

Acknowledgements

To the Martyrs of the Word of God so that others would smell the fragrance of love that I have known, and love flamboyantly.

~C. L. Thomas

To God be the glory, who taught the prophets to bear the fruit of the heart, the evidence of love.

Narration

The days were dark and cold; rain without sun. The light in the lamps grew dim. There was pain all around. Darkness grew on the earth and it chilled the bones. Through the darkness you could see shadows of mercy, answers to the pleas of the earth.

Darkness grew on the earth like shafts of wheat in a field with no end. The wind would blow the wheat. It was the wind of destruction. It blew the wheat until it bent and broke. The wind of destruction blew the wheat until it rolled together into a bundle and then blew it to the four corners of the earth. There, the bundles would then be tied with strands of lies and deceit.

The field of wheat stubble was all that remained on the earth. The fields of the earth were gleaned and barren by the wind of destruction. The wheat stubble still shined in the sun, breaks still reflecting the light. The sun rose fierce upon the fields of barren wheat stubble. It was the Father's fury; it was the Father's wrath. There would not be a new planting; there would not be a new crop. The fields of the earth would no longer bear a harvest for the wind of destruction.

For the Lord had promised He would no longer destroy the earth and its inhabitants for the cause of wickedness. He was the author of life, a God of beginnings and not ends. His love would be nurtured and live because He is a God rich in mercy and powerful in love. He had plans to subdue the enemy and plans to fulfill His own purposes.

In the moments of these late hours of the earth, His mercy was rich in the power of love. He is a God rich in mercy. His richness had afforded Him a Son. His Son was His prized possession, His medal of honor, and His symbol of love to the earth.

He taught His Son to ride above the earth; close to His heart until He reached His final destination arrived. Clothed in white He is seated next to the Father: The worthy White Rider.

In the fullness of His love for the earth He will ride again. In His love for mankind His necessary talents will be summoned, for He is the hope of the nations to the four corners of the earth. In the mercy of God, He will be summoned the worthy White Rider to the earth; to touch the hearts of mankind and teach them to ride, victoriously. This is the end time prophecy of the worthy White Rider.

> *Many shall be purified, and made white, and tried; but the wicked shall do wickedly and none of the wicked shall understand; but the wise shall understand.* (Daniel 12:10)

Chapter 1

The Days Were Dark

I was seated in the holy heavenly throne room. I saw through a portal what appeared to be four large fishermen's nets over the earth. There was no land on the earth that was not covered by these huge nets. They were staked along the top edges. They surrounded each nation and then dropped down passed the earth, the net's bottom hanging just out of sight of the earth's inhabitants. It was staked over the earth; covering and holding the people. Unaware Of their danger, the people would drop down one at a time through the net and would be caught at the bottom of the net below the earth like fish being caught in a fisherman's net.

The people caught in the nets below the earth were within the grasp of demons. The demons would reach through the nets to torment and twist the "catch" of people. They were caught in the grasp of their torment of destruction. They would struggle, but the pull of the weight of the nets was too tight. They struggled against humanity. I could see them reach out from inside the nets to escape the accumulation of people within. They struggled against themselves and the lies they believed. They were confused about what was the truth. They believed the enemy was themselves, each other, and didn't see the true enemy that kept out of their view. Screams couldn't be heard to the world from the bottom of the fishermen's net. They couldn't be heard to save even one as they dropped to join those already caught and captured.

The whole earth was covered in the nets of lies and deception. As each man battled for a kingdom of self that didn't exist, they forfeited the truth for lies and were under the power and control of deception.

They pulled at the stakes driven into the earth keeping them within the nets, only to realize the stakes were too large and too long for humanity to remove. They could get the stakes to move and wobble a bit, but the stakes were in the depths of immovability. Their strength against the stakes only left them weary.

The hour was near; a change had come. It didn't come from the east. It didn't come from the west. It came from the heart. The Father had left a key, so to speak. It wasn't from the earth; it was from the place where they were conceived. It spoke of hope and heaven. It spoke of triumph and power. They sang a new song from underneath the nets. It rose from the strands and chords of wickedness; a song of dreams and freedom under nets of poverty and plagues. The Father's mercy and love fell on them through the nets. His glory shown like sunshine on a rainy day, breaking through the nets to bring them discernment to perceive the boundaries of their forfeit.

They would unite their hearts and conform in the power of the love within their hearts. Together they would lift a section of the net and experience relief from it. But they could not break free from the net. They resembled the world in their antics and struggles that came from within themselves for refuge; amidst a control that was without remedy, without promise. They perceived the truth but were powerless to live it. They cried out for the truth with hearts of self. Love was something they perceived in their hearts for their own benefit, for their own kingdoms.

But the Father saw differently. The Father saw a world captured by the enemy. He saw the whole earth under the sway of the wicked one. They were under his sway, his power and his control. He infiltrated their way of life, their mindsets, even their worship was within his timing and his grasp.

Their sacredness amounted to stolen moments of the heart. The Lord began to build an army of those who would steal away with Him to hear the truth; His End Time Army, His lovers of the truth. They would steal away moments from the world; stolen moments of love, truth, power and revelation. Revelation of God, revelation of humanity and revelation of the enemy.

Chapter 2

The Wind of Destruction

From the throne room I was allowed another glimpse of the world as the Father sees it, in its peril. I could see the four large fishermen's nets over the nations and the people dropping down to be caught out of sight and sound below the earth. I could also see a fortified city resting above the clouds, just above the earth on the opposite end of the catch of people below within nets.

The fortressed city was erected with elaborate architecture, glistening and with purpose. It stood a magnificent kingdom with boundaries resting not too far from the circumference of the earth, unseen by its captives below the clouds. In the center of this second heaven Kingdom I saw a palace. It was grand with steps that lead to columns, a portrait of an official government building. There was a throne within.

The Lord said, "That's where the enemy sat."

He ruled from this position in this magnificent city, dusting the earth with his power and suggestions. They were covered in the lies of their forfeit. They had relinquished power to him, he subdued the nations with this power and the rein of his glory.

The earth's inhabitants were his puppets on a string and he played them against each other. The puppets all played a part in the service to his kingdom above the earth. He held their destiny like puppets on a string. He ruled above the nets and called himself the Grand Master.

He ruled over them with power and authority, and knowledge of the heavenly kingdom above, with permission of the saints of glory. He ruled over them with the power God had given His sons and daughters of the earth, and ruled with the selfishness he had taught them with his lies to perform his will.

The Grand Master sat comfortably on his throne in the middle of his bright city; his kingdom above the earth. He's suited as a man, crowned and across his lap was a scepter. The earth is colorless and so are the captives below it in comparison to the brilliant colorful kingdom that enthrones its ruler.

Looking towards the gray earth I could see a woman reaching out from beneath the net. You could hear her cries of affliction and brokenness. The Grand Master rises from his throne and points the end of his scepter towards the earth. A portal opens to allow him to observe the panic of her struggle against his nets. Anyone caught struggling against the nets causes him to spin in a whirlwind of fury and manifest himself in the form of a winged dragon. He then flies through the portal, pointing the end of his speared tail in the direction of the disturbance. He pierces them through the nets and forces them back down to the earth, unheard and unseen by those not yet captured. He flies around the earth looking for any other offenders ready to strike them with the end of his tail until he regains control of the atmosphere. Satisfied, he rises above the earth and resumes his throne.

The Grand Master on his throne has subdued the nations. He is victorious over the world and rules and reigns with the authority that has been relinquished to him. He has risen above the clouds of the air of humanity as the only breath they breathe. He has moved into the place of authority that the hearts of men have abandoned to him. He has risen in vanity and in the power of his own will. He has captivated his captives in the reflections of his likeness. Blinded by deception, caught in pride, and plagued with vanity, they dance to his drum as they sing his song and become drunk with his wine. Dwelling on the earth, they are being robbed of family and are plagued with the un-holiness of self will.

Chapter 3

The Lake of the Gallows

As I sat in the throne room this morning, Jesus cautioned me on the magnitude of today's vision as I now caution you.

Visiting with the Father, Jesus opened before me a portal that allowed me to see into the center of the enemy's kingdom in the second heaven. We were positioned above his palace and given vision of the inside of the palace where I saw three thrones.

The enemy known as the Grand Master sat on the center throne of his elaborate palace. He was a light complexioned man, dressed in a business suit and red tie. An elongated crown was positioned on his head and a scepter lay across his arm rests. He wore a dark purple velvet robe and a long gold necklace in the shape of a satanic star was around his neck. To his right sat a hairy creature with eyes that glared with red fury. Its head was like a vulture but the beak was elongated and seemed larger than that of a normal vulture and was filled with jagged shark like teeth. He had arms of skin like a strong muscle man, his belly looked like a bear and his feet were as bear claws. He sat upright on his throne. To the enemy's left, a scarcely dressed lustful woman sat seductively on her throne with eyes that flowed with a black glow. When she moved she slithered like a snake.

Two demons blanketed in all black shadows came into the palace before the Grand Master. They were dragging a naked man, one to an arm and thrust before the throne landing on his hands and knees for judgment.

"What are the charges and offenses laid against him?" the Grand Master asked the demons.

"He has transgressed against your laws and bylaws. He has lived a life that has refused to worship you, has not bowed to your name, nor assembled for its cause. He has lived a life unto himself my lord, occasionally bowing to the enemy," exclaims the demon.

The Grand Master rose and began to pace in front of the naked man saying, "I will help him remember who the true lord is. He will not forget I am lord this time, take him to the gallows!"

The naked man is taken to a courtyard and harnessed to a pole exposing his back. The demons use the cat-of-nine-tails whips on him until the blood flows from every area of skin accessible to the whip. The man is then made to carry his gallows up a designated hill in the second heaven. Two others in skeleton form with little flesh are already crucified there, but still the spirit within them is able to move the skull to notice the addition. The demons nail him to the cross between the other two. The crows are waiting near by to light on his flesh, the area being deemed for a daily crow feeding ritual.

The Grand Master attends the ceremony to view the fresh crucifixion. Seeing his orders carried out he proceeds down the hill towards his throne, blood flowing in a stream towards the heels of his shoes. The blood flows faster than he walks and streams past him to a lake of blood at the bottom of the hill. He tracks blood into the palace leading to his throne. The Grand Master sits on his throne, examining his shoes coated with blood.

It begins to trouble him and he calls out, "Counselor!"

A man, whom I sensed was Judas, comes from an office behind the throne. It's an official looking room surrounded in cherry wood décor. A large laptop could be seen sitting on the executive, cherry wood desk.

His counselor answers, "Yes my lord and king."

"Why has this blood been left on my shoes and in my palace?" questions the Grand Master.

"Fresh blood reminds you of <u>the</u> crucifixion that deemed you victorious over the enemy, my lord and king," replies his counselor.

"And now it no longer is fresh and I want it cleaned and removed from my presence; put it in the sewer where it belongs," the Grand Master exclaims.

"Yes, my lord and king," says the counselor as he excuses himself to quickly summon two demons with a bucket and towels.

The demons towel the blood off his shoes and make their way towards the palace doors mopping up the blood from the throne room's golden pathway and wringing it in a bucket. Finished, they pour the bucket of cooled blood to the lake of blood at the bottom of the hill of the gallows.

Chapter 4

The Four Corners of the Earth

The Holy Spirit and I, unseen in a corner of the ceiling in the Grand Master's palace, followed him around as he walked through the palace doors to a covered balcony supported by scrolled columns. There the Holy Spirit reassured me that the enemy was afraid of Him and that I was not to worry. I was safe and unseen. Once on the palace balcony, the earth was clearly revealed through a portal. The Grand Master looked routinely towards the earth as in surveillance. Suddenly, an angel moving as a lighting bolt came across his sight from heaven towards earth and caught his attention.

Minutes later a few others darted to the earth causing his anger to explode as he screams, "Counselor!"

His counselor appears, wearing a signet ring and carrying a lap top under his arm, "yes, my lord and king?"

"What is the meaning of these angelic trespassers? They are going against my laws. I have subdued the earth and the inhabitants belong to me. I rule the earth," the Grand Master exclaims."

His counselor responds, "The God of Light has sent them claiming the earth is His."

The Grand Master angrily declares, "He gave the earth to its inhabitants and they belong to me!"

Opening his laptop, the counselor presents a screen depicting the conquered areas on the earth, "You have subdued these nations and they worship you in all these regions."

He points to black spots covering the influential densely populated areas on the earth saying, "They even worship you in blood sacrifice in these areas. And now even more of the prayers of the Buddhist are going towards your will my lord."

"It is a feeble attempt to subdue the nations. He couldn't possibly take back the whole earth for they belong to me. I have the earth and its fullness," the Grand Master exclaims.

The Grand Master notices four light grey areas on the screen depicting the four corners on the earth and asks, "What of these?"

"These four corners are waiting on you my lord; then you will subdue the whole earth. There are but few worshipers of the enemy in place on these four corners. They cannot be compared to your sheer numbers, my lord king," Judas says in council.

"I will take my worshipers to the four corners of the earth and I will not rest until it is mine. Prepare for my rise and my reign," the Grand Master orders.

Chapter 5

Storming the Enemy's Camp

Seated in the throne room the Father opens a portal of the second heaven kingdom, revealing the enemy's camp. The Holy Spirit invites me to join Him through the portal today to storm the enemy's camp. This is the eyewitness account of the enemy's battle plan from the third heaven. Please be aware of its graphic content.

The Order of Offense

I saw the enemy's counselor, Judas of Iscariot, typing out orders from the Grand Master. His office is stationed behind the throne and contains computer monitors mounted to the wall with images viewing each side of the earth, black indicating their dominance. Also in the counselor's office is a sophisticated communication system which links his office to all areas of the kingdom. He is typing out an email on his lap top to the demons and to the Grand Master's end time army.

From the monitor, it reads as follows:

"You have been summoned and ordered on this day by the Grand Master's appointed, to march on the earth's four corners in these gray areas I have outlined. The horsemen are ordered to suit up. They are ordered to ride fierce and drive out the enemy. The grey areas are currently under subjection to the light. This light hinders the king's wishes and will. You are here by notified; this is no longer permitted nor to be tolerated by the wishes and order of his Majesty. For this grave attempt to overthrow his power and his right, given to him through the inhabitants now covering the earth, is an offense against the Grand Master's kingdom. And the God of Light is in violation of his Majesty's rule. The earth will be subdued in its entirety for the will and purposes of his Majesty. Those in violation of this order of offense will be retaliated against in unmerciful abandonment by order of the king. Let his worshipers of the earth be notified and may we rise in unity to the high call of the will of his Majesty."

~Grand Master
Signet Seal.

When Judas has finished preparing the document, he walks from his office behind the throne to bring the sealed scroll before the Grand Master.

"You're law, Master," says his counselor.

"I will subdue the earth in its fullness; the enemy is powerless to stop me. This will be their last attempt to overthrow me! I am god, the people belong to me," the Grand Master exclaims.

The dark king glares at the lighter gray areas on the documents in the four corners of the earth with fire in his eyes and exclaims, "Trespassers! I will overtake the enemy on the four corners of light if I have to do it myself! I have done it once before, no one can stop me!"

He moves from his throne to view the portal of the earth below and declares, "God of Light, I render you powerless against me! I will overtake the earth because I have transformed your light into darkness. You lose, and I am the victorious one!"

Thrusting his scepter horizontally in the air towards heaven, the dark King shouts; "Ready your troops for battle. I will rise and not fall. Prepare for battle oh heavens for the battle. You will not overpower me for this is the battle to the end."

Looking towards the earth, he crosses his arms and proclaims, "I am king. I have always been king, and I will forever be, king of the earth. Their attempts to overthrow me from generation to generation have failed. They will utterly fall. I am the master, the Grand Master over the earth. I am their Lord. I am the one who does, I am the one that did, and I am the one that will have!"

Chapter 6

The Lord Promised

The portal from the throne room today revealed a highlighted area where a black fort has been built on stilts appearing to be on one of the four lighter gray corners of the earth; the East. As the Holy Spirit and I drew closer to the earth, I saw it was an enemy fort, black like the occupants inside. One evil being was holding a telescope and wearing a commander's hat. He had demons accompanying him. The fort contained a black flag with a purple satanic star and an empty scroll cylinder. They were encamped about near a portal of light that reached to the third heavens and contained one white warrior inside.

The warrior was kneeling and praying to the Holy, Father God. He was wearing a thick full bodied armor, a knight's suit; his or her identity was undetectable. The warrior was accompanied by angels moving to and from heaven within the light portal that resembled a light beam stretching from heaven to earth. The warrior was known to heaven as a Rider on the earth; a warrior in the Lord's End Time Army. The angels strengthened him as he prayed and polished his armor as to shine and to keep it free from any dust of the earth.

The dark commander, disturbed by what he saw, paced the portals circumference, seeming to control its boundaries and secure ground that was not in the light. While the warrior was praying, I saw an angel descending and carrying a scroll with a message for him. It was an invitation from the risen saints and the risen prophets of who now reside in the holiness of heaven.

*The Invitation

"We, the prophets of old, who foretold of the coming King, join our swords in unity with the End Time Army. Swords drawn, not of ourselves, but in alliance and honor to the Lion who has defeated the enemy and will roar into victory! Our swords are raised as part of the End Time Army! Hail to the coming King! He will come to the earth as a Lion and will establish His victory in righteousness."

"Our swords are drawn," says the saints of old, "and they will not meet their sheaths until the Lord

God's will be done, for we will be partakers in the wedding feast of the Lion and the Lamb."

"May the prophets of old and the End Time Army be united in the power of love just as our King and His son are united in the power of Love."

~The Risen Prophets

*The Invitation is an excerpt from the book <u>Memoirs: Reflections of the Father's Heart</u>, also of the author C. L. Thomas.

Chapter 7

The Saluted Swords of Heaven

The warrior within the light pulls the sword carried behind him from ifs sheath and lifts it above his head towards heaven. Then I could see several spirit swords from heaven come down from the top of the light portal, tip first, and touch the tip of his vertical sword and then unite at the handles. Power fell on the warrior's sword. Power flowed from the unity of the drawn swords. A swirl of power came down around the warrior, filled with the honor, strength and devotion of those who lived and died unto love. The angels came and joined in the honor of the whirlwind of the unified power of love from heaven to earth. I saw the angels take a gold chord and wrap it around the drawn saluting swords, wrapping them together with the warrior's sword until they came together as one. The warrior's sword now contained and symbolized the strength of the swords of heaven's prophets, including that of the prophet of prophets. It was now one brilliant, strong, united symbolic weapon.

The warrior, feeling the weight of his unified sword, seems humbled at the power it represented and knelt asking that the Lord's will be done in and through it. As the prayer went up, the angels came down bringing a cloak of white and draping it over his shoulders. He lifts his bowed head to find the light portal he's within surrounded by an army of darkness.

The Encompassed Dark Army

I saw demons carrying swords and riding wolves with red eyes, ready to pounce on the light warrior. I saw witches and warlocks of the earth, swords drawn, on wolves ready to move into this portal of light surrounding God's end time warrior. Suddenly, a single demon riding a wolf pierces the light and then begins to yelp. The warrior reacts, making a sudden, swift motion with the unified sword slicing the wolf's head off. Unprepared for the electrifying power of the portal, the weakened demon moves in contortions as to advance on the warrior but its strength has been sapped. He joins the pieces of his wolf on the outer side of the light.

The warrior cleans the blood of his unified sword and tosses the bloody cloth outside the light portal.

News traveled quickly to the Grand Master's throne and riles him. He orders His counselor to immediately take another dictation saying, "A casualty has been reported in the Grand Master's army. A wolf in defense of his territory has been beheaded by the sword of the enemy. He has gone with honors. This casualty will not go unnoticed and we will redefine our tactics and strategy in the future. No lone wolves are to advance. We advance now as one. The enemy may have won this battle but we will win the war. Prepare to advance as one. I have spoken."

~Grand Master
Signet Seal

The Grand Master, growing in anger at the thought of his enemy's powerful sword, grabs the fresh scroll holding his newly dictated orders and exclaims to Judas, "Give it to me I will take it to the commander myself!"

The Grand Master moves down the portal towards the earth with great speed, once again transformed into a winged dragon. The dragon form clutches the side of the dark fort, scroll in his claws, and glares at the fear struck dark commander. At first I could not understand when the winged dragon spoke. It sounded like a rumbling roar, but then my hearing cleared and I could clearly hear the exchange.

"What are these reports of casualties coming before my throne commander?" he roared then threw the scroll at the commander. "See that these new orders are carried out."

He blew fire into the sky before he departed to fly to his throne through the dark portal. Small fires start all around the commander's fort. The demons rush to extinguish them.

The warrior in the midst of the light portal notices a great army of demons and satanic worshipers on wolves with more coming up behind them on warriors on black horses. He lowers himself in a crouched defensive position with the unified sword outstretched as he sees the magnitude of the great, dark, army that has risen up against him.

An angel comes down and speaks a spirit of peace over the warrior. His body begins to release the fear that had tried to grip his flesh and he stands upright again, ready to do battle for the souls of men.

Chapter 8

The Battle of Souls

I see Jesus come down the portal, face the white warrior and put His hands on the warrior's shoulders.

"Do you see this army before you, My beloved?" Jesus asks as He points to the great dark army.

"Yes, I see," says the warrior.

"They are not against you, they are not against your flesh, nor are they against the love that we share so deeply," Jesus says as He points to heaven. "They're against God's light on the earth because it's a threat to their very existence. I'm God's Son, you are God's child. The enemy isn't satisfied with the earth; he wants to take God's children with him."

"You are in *The Battle of Soul's* great warrior," Jesus says and strokes the warrior's head lovingly. "You will fight for your right to life. You will go more valiantly then I rode, your sword is the sword of the martyrs who lived and died for the love of God."

"Today, great united warrior, I crown you with life for defending the honor of it," Jesus says and takes off His crown and places it on the warrior's head.

Then glory falls from His crown showering the warrior's armor with light as a robe and a white cloaked and crown warrior emerges.

You can hear the dark army, the gnashing of teeth and growls coming from just outside the light portal.

Jesus grabs the hand of the warrior that's holding the unified sword, lifts it up to heaven and rotates His spirit into the warrior's. The warrior now unified with Jesus emerges as the worthy White Rider.

The White Rider, God made into flesh once again, says, "We move as one! We move as one heart, as one mind, as one spirit of love unto God."

Jesus' spirit radiates from within the warrior's armor now.

"We ride to the nations," Jesus says as He lifts their unified sword towards the battle, "in unity with the kingdom risen saints, martyrs and prophets."

He salutes saying, "We ride to release the captives and set the prisoners free, to heal the broken hearted and to proclaim the coming of the Lord. This is the new day, not unto ourselves, but unto God and His family. For life is in unity with Me and to die for the cause of God's family is to profit."

The Equipped Enabled Heart of the Warrior

The warrior's enabled heart, molded by the love of his Father has equipped his heart to unite with Jesus' heart. In oneness of spirit and heart they grip the sword, skillfully ushering in the holiness of heaven and creating a light force of power that reaches from the sword into heaven. His words begin to usher in His commands.

Suddenly, a huge horse as swift as lightening is loosed from heaven. The sword has opened heaven and released its accumulated and awaited treasure. The horse, a magnificent white creature made for victory, has moved underneath the White Rider as if it knows its master's spirit.

"We ride as one," shouts Jesus unified within the warrior's armor and holding the unified sword toward heaven.

The front hooves of His white horse rise up with the White Rider on its back, as if in allegiance to heaven, a familiar position. The horse's eyes gleam of white light and amber fire. The strands of gold collected from heaven shimmer on the longer hair above its hooves. His mane and tail sparkle with flecks of white gems as if he's been running on the shores of the crystal sea in heaven. The saddle under the overshadowed White Rider reads: "King of Kings Lord of Lords" with a gem stone in the center. The white horse has a garland around his neck, with the adornment of heaven in the style of a Native American motif.

The White Rider proclaims, "Father, let it be unto me on earth as it is in heaven. Let Your will be done!"

Angels begin to fly from heaven down the swords light beam like a slide. Once on the earth, just inside the light portal the angels encircle the perimeter as a barrier, with their arms folded. After the angels descend, it appeared as if a large corral gate has been opened in heaven. I saw a multitude of white horses thundering from heaven and enlarging the portal as they formed a single line on each side of the White Rider, in perfect formation as if rehearsed.

After the horses, I saw risen saints and prophets move down the light portal as if the sword beckoned them. The prophets came down one at time and addressed the White Rider on the great white horse, Jesus within the earthly man.

They each bowed, stated their name and said, "I ride with you, Jesus."

Then they mounted white horses, side-by-side as a frontline. The risen prophets were familiar as they bowed and announced their intentions to ride.

I heard John, Paul, Timothy, Mark, Luke and Peter announce they would ride with Jesus. There were thousands of familiar and unfamiliar martyrs of the faith that mounted their horses, side-by-side enlarging the width of the portal as far as the eye could see.

Chapter 9

The Great Army of the Lord

"We, the great Army of the Lord, risen saints and prophets, move this day in unity with our hearts interlinked by one heart and one spirit, in one mind unto the Lord. On this day, by the heart beat of heaven, we move forward as the great Army of the Lord, advancing in great honor, power and unity with the Lord of life. We move as one. No one leads and no one follows. We are without rank or titles as we march together with honor as a family in the power and unity of the love bestowed on us from heaven, our holy destination. Marked by heaven we advance, Kingdom Knights of Valor, for victory has been bought by the Lamb and is our right and possession."

"Hear ye! Hear ye! To those embattled against us for the souls captured in the lies of deceit: We have heard the cries for mercy that have come before the throne and are here for and march on behalf of those fallen without hope. And in accordance to the dictates of the book of <u>Revelation</u>, we ride unto the four corners of the earth! We ride to free the captives. We ride to release the prisoners. We ride with the authority of Heaven for it is written: The earth is the Lord's and the fullness there of (Psalm 24:1). This day we battle for souls. We will cut the captives free from your plans of darkness, that justice may prevail. We are one, united for the truth of mercy, the truth of justice, and the truth of life!"

The Holy Spirit and I passed the empty corrals in heaven today, where once I had seen white horses pressing on the gate, anticipating its opening as if they knew their destination and purpose. Down the light portal to earth they had gone forming a front line on each side of the White Rider, the warrior with Jesus within his heart and spirit. Now they stretched as far as the eye could see having enlarged the light portal as the risen saints, suited and armed to ride, mounted on the horse's of heaven.

The White Rider now faces a dark warrior positioned just outside the portal. The dark warrior wears two swords on his back and one at his side. His black armor looks old as if he has lived in it for years and he carries a scroll. He rides a black horse. The atmosphere around them seemed cold as I could see the breath of the horse's nostrils. The horse's eyes were red with a wild look in them.

The black warrior holds his unrolled scroll in front of him as he faces the White Rider and says, "Trespassers!"

The White Rider quotes a verse from the Bible in reply, "The earth is the Lord's and the fullness thereof" (Psalm 24:1).

At this declaration, the angels that have surrounded the circumference of the light portal begin to push the wolves back with their persistent stance and glory until the wolves are scarce.

The black warrior has brought forward a large bundle of captive people within a fisherman's net. They are fear stricken, scarcely dressed; dirty men and women with barely room to move. The black warrior places the bundles of people in front of his frontline of dark horses, using them as a barricade.

With the bundle now in front of him he says, "If you wish to move forward, you must move through these!"

We Ride for Love, We Ride for Family, We Ride for Victory

The dark warrior speaks to the White Rider from the other side of the light portal saying, "What kind of rider are you? Are you one that tramples over men with the hooves of heaven?"

The dark army laughs as their leader continues, "Or are you the prophesied one to take away the sins of the whole earth? Look, we've made it easy for you and brought them to you."

More bundles of people, including older children who are bloodied and weary in body and spirit, are placed on each side of his black horse.

The White Rider's stance and countenance does not change.

"I am here for what belongs to Me and My Father who sent Me," replies the White Rider. "We are one and We are many!"

"Prophets foretell their end on the earth and write about it on their way out," laughs the dark warrior. "You're nothing that hasn't come before you or after you. You are but another tear in my uniform. What's it going to be prophet?"

The White Rider looks him in the eyes and says with the strength of a unified heart, "We ride! We ride for love, we ride for family, we ride for victory, for it is written; 'the kingdom of heaven suffereth violence, and the violent take it by force'"(Matthew 11:12).

Chapter 10

At One With the White Rider

The Holy Spirit and I flow to the earth through the light portal to find the Lord's End Time Army at its base. Today the Holy Spirit anchors me with the belt of truth to the White Rider as I assume the position of the warrior saddled on Jesus' white horse, ready to confront and face the enemy's leader. My spirit joins the spirit of Jesus in one heart with the ones I love in the spiritual realm. The Holy Spirit sitting behind me asks me to lift the sword the White Rider holds in his hand.

As I lift the sword in unity with Jesus, as the warrior White Rider, I feel heaven in the sword. I have Jesus' warm heart of love filling my heart as if the family of God's love is flowing from heaven within my spirit and with the saints on either side of us. It is their strength within the sword. I can see and feel Father God's head nod with approval.

I am secure in His blessing and with the strength of heaven I lift the sword representing heaven on earth.

> *When I have bent Judah for me, filled the bow with Ephraim, and rose up thy sons, O Zion, against thy sons, O Greece, and made thee as the sword of a mighty man. And the LORD shall be seen over them, and his arrow shall go forth as the lightning: and the Lord GOD shall blow the trumpet, and shall go with whirlwinds of the south. he LORD of hosts shall defend them; and they shall devour, and subdue with sling stones; and they shall drink, [and] make a noise as through wine; and they shall be filled like bowls, [and] as the corners of the altar. And the LORD their God shall save them in that day as the flock of his people: for [they shall be as] the stones of a crown, lifted up as an ensign upon his land. For how great [is] his goodness, and how great [is] his beauty! corn shall make the young men cheerful, and new wine the maids.* (Zechariah 9:13-17)

The White Rider rides with the spirit, heart and strength of a family. The unified sword comes down and it is held across the front of the horn on the saddle, as to rest comfortably in the assurance of the many that the White Rider represents; heaven on earth aligned in one place. As peace that surpasses all understanding abides within the light portal, we hear the screams of the people still caught within fishermen's nets that have been placed between the frontline of the dark riders and that of the White Rider.

The dark warrior finds his confidence in his stance and rides his horse around the additional bundles of suffering people that have been placed on each side of him. Then he draws one of the two long sickle-like swords hanging from his back.

As he lifts his sword towards heaven, he declares the sword, "The Prophet Killer."

The dark riders lift their swords in preparation for battle. At the same time, as if a starting gun was fired at a race track, the white horses simultaneously rise up their front legs and advance over the top of the dark horses' heads throwing the dark riders off their horses.

The white horses throw the dark riders off the black horses with their hooves while White Riders quickly cut the nets releasing the captives. Once the large white horses have thrown off the dark riders, they kicked their back hooves to keep the dark animals down and then to break their necks. The white horses seem to have the ability to discern the enemy as well as to fly.

However, the captives seem to be spiritually blindfolded giving them a limited understanding of the battle going on all around them. As the dark riders moved away to save themselves from the beating hooves of the white horses, they gathered a few of the freed captives who move towards them in the wrong direction. The dark riders hold them captive once more by holding a large sword at their necks hoping to protect themselves from the White Riders.

Chapter 11

Freedom to the Captives

Most of the freed captives were being pulled inside the light portal by the angels who then breathed life into their faint spirits as if giving them spiritual CPR. Some of the freed captives ran in the wrong direction, away from the light portal. Angels went after them, administering the breath of life and pointing them the way they should go. Without the breath of life, the captives possessed spirits that blinded their spiritual eyes making them unable to perceive the spirit realm or discern their own spiritual demise. They've lived lives of captivity, imprisoned by spiritual lack, possessing only the knowledge of God's love without ever perceiving the power of living within that love. They were born and bred in captivity therefore their knowledge of love could not free them. Once they were cut free by the unity of love within God's family, the angels escorted them up the light portal into the throne room to encounter their Maker.

Free to Love, Again

From the throne room in the third heaven, the Holy Spirit and I could see the freed captives sit on the Father's lap, one by one. We could hear the Father speak to each one of them saying:

"You are home where you belong, where you were created in the image of God. You are mine, created by Me for Me to love. I have raptured you this day by the power of love. I have raptured you back this day from the grips of death that you would know the freedom that you deserve to know. You were brought back to Me today by a family of love. A family of love that believes you are valuable and precious. The truth is you are a part of a great family that could not or will not, ever forget you. I am your Father, I believe in the love you once knew. You have all the love you need to sustain you all the time, every moment of the day because I say so; whether you believe it or not."

"I will make you a promise that if you follow Me and remain in Me you will continue to receive life and will live with Me forever. Beloved, remain in Me and I will see to it that your darkness is turned into light. As you remain in Me you will become as light just as I am and suffer darkness no more. I send you with My blessing, My child. Be of good cheer; for I have overcome the world," the Father says.

The Father sheds a tear as He releases His children to the angels who escort them back down the portal to their earthly dwellings where they will awake to a new day as the sun comes in their windows from a night of peaceful sleep.

Chapter 12

Victory is as Sweet as Honey

The *Battle of Souls* has ended. It was an eerie feeling as I returned to the scene of the recent battle and rejoined the White Rider in spirit. The dark warrior and his army had drawn back without the leverage of the bundles of hostages. Empty nets lay next to the dying dark horses that once appeared as equals confronting the front line of white horses.

"We, many as one, lift the unified sword that released the captive spirits to their Father. We now proclaim victory," exclaims the Lord's End Time Army.

Holding the sword high, standing on top of the dying dark horses, our hearts as one begin to sing, "Victory is sweet and pleasant like honey in the honeycomb, pure goodness. This day the bounty is the Lord's. Hail to the King! His victory is sure, and His words are pure; like honey from the honeycomb.

May His bounty be plentiful to His bosom; for He is worthy of the love of His children. Hail to the King! All hail to His holiness, His truth has prevailed. Let all declare His praises. Let His victory be known in the praises of His people who have been loosed from their prison. He wants to hear them singing His praise from the earth, from end to end!"

Chapter 13

The Favor of Your Love

The Lord's Army moves back off the dark horses. As the White Rider dismounts His white horse, Jesus separates Himself as a sign to the Warrior that He must return to His place beside the Father. The Warrior silently bows before Jesus.

"You have My honor," Jesus says. "My love will live in your heart forever, faithful friend."

The warrior replies, "As You will, my dear Lord."

"This day I crown you with My love," Jesus says taking off His crown and placing it on the Warrior's head.

"This day you are awarded My sword, oh mighty man of valor. Live your life and ride high in the power of the faith and love of a heavenly family. Let Us hear the sound of your horse's hooves, until your horse is corralled and you join Us in heaven. You are My good and faithful White Rider," says Jesus as He begins to depart up the light portal towards heaven.

"We are just a whisper away to a heart that is pure. Ride near to the heartbeat of heaven, We will be listening. Don't be afraid, your heart knows the way. Love can never be separated or divided, but lives as one heartbeat," says Jesus as His form fades to white.

The White Rider looks at his undefeated sword, overwhelmed with the love it represents. To be near to his friend Jesus and the love they shared was where the White Rider wanted to be, where the largest piece of his heart would be complete. The world had lost its appeal and there was nothing left but to decline it. To be made alive by the atmosphere of heaven, to live the life that comes with the oil of heaven and to please the Father's heart by answering His every call was where the White Rider needed to abide.

To know his Father's ears would be listening for the sound of his horse's hooves riding near to His heart would be as music to His ears until their next face-to-face. The Father, the Son, the risen saints, the angels, and the family of God have taught the Warrior the power of love unified. He chooses to remain on the earth to teach others the way to love unified. The family of God taught him in the spirit of love, the will of God.

Chapter 14

Teach Them to Ride

I arrived in the third heaven on horse back today, soon after *the Battle of Souls.* As I dismounted, an angel took the reigns and I moved to where Jesus welcomed the White Rider. He is ready to teach the White Rider the way to abide in love and to ride high, knowing the desires of the Rider's heart. I too wait eagerly, ready to listen to the teacher of teachers, the talented one. Before He begins, Jesus hands me a gold pen and tells me to take notes as He speaks from the throne room.

Jesus begins to quote the way of high riders. As He speaks, I eagerly write down everything He says about how to ride high above the world and abide in the atmosphere of heaven.

Jesus begins by teaching, "The Cardinal Rules of Riders."

"1st Cardinal Rule~We stay together. Whenever you ride you'll be riding with Me and the risen saints. There is a place for the riders of the earth near to the throne room as to be heard from heaven's floor. Decline the world and the tactics of the enemy. Ride in unity with the Kingdom. Maturity wears the truth proudly. Take Me with you in your heart and don't let go. That's the honor I'm looking for. So shall I be with you. Ride High.

2nd Cardinal Rule~Let love live within your heart. Abide close to heaven and be ready when the Lord calls your name for instruction in righteousness.

3rd Cardinal Rule~Live to teach God's love, the fulfillment of the law. Ride high to be of service to the King, to teach love.

4th Cardinal Rule~Love the Lord God with all your heart, and with all your soul, and with your entire mind, and with all your strength. Prefer the mind of Christ. Prefer to hold heaven in your heart above all. Pray atonement to allow your atmosphere to be holy and find your strength in the atmosphere of the love of God.

And thou shalt love the Lord thy God with all thy heart, and with all thy soul, and with all thy mind, and with all thy strength: this [is] the first commandment. And the second [is] like, [namely] this, Thou shalt love thy neighbour as thyself. There is none other commandment greater than these. (Mark 12:30-31 KJV)

5th Cardinal Rule~Leave a trail for the lost. Lead by example; lead with love, live by faith and sacrifice all for the Father's will. Live as a treasure in an earthen vessel. No longer live as apart of the world, live to glorify God as a piece of a kingdom family on the earth. Live a life to glorify your kingdom family on the earth; live as one, love as one, do not live in fear."

"Let us hear your horse's hooves as you ride, even at the door," says Jesus.

But we have this treasure in earthen vessels, that the excellency of the power may be of God, and not of us. (2 Corinthians 4:7)

The Rider's Place

Sitting in heaven in the place for the Rider today the Holy Spirit and I began to prepare me to absorb the lessons Jesus had taught. This place was just below the throne room and beautiful just as heaven is beautiful. Angels guard the rights of access. This place of purpose and of identity can only be reached with my heart as I remain in the love by breathing the atmosphere of heaven. It is here in love's secure warm safe embrace that I can take spiritual breaths of life and be in perfect peace as I am unified by one mind and one heart in one atmosphere of love and heavenly family. As I hold onto heaven, I tangibly receive gifts from God that reveal my true identity and enable me to perform God's will for me. He gives spiritual tools and advice that which enabling me to perform the mandates He has given me to release blessings over my earthly and heavenly family and bring a return of supernatural blessings to the earth. For family, heavenly and earthly family.

This is a place in heaven honors my heart in big and small ways. I find my children's beloved goldfish that have passed away living happily here. I see large memorials and fountain statues of spiritual accomplishments in my honor and replicates our love. It offers a gathering place for a more intimate heavenly family that is familiar with the purposes and mandates over me. The tabernacle table is full of the bounty of heaven, heavenly food for feasting.

Chapter 15

The Rider's Song

I have sought the Lord's love as my greatest treasure and I have known intimate places shared with the Holy Spirit. He has taught me of myself, the reality of what God created me to be and how He has loved me, always. In His embrace I feel peace and love and my spirit remembers His touch; calm and gentle, familiar, where I am known. He fastens the belt of truth enabling me to ride. I ride near Him because of the love we share and the love I've known when I dwell within heaven, within His spirit as He dwells within mine. We are inseparable because of love. We prefer the atmosphere of life and the goodness of the love for the Father. I know to do His will always involves my best interest.

I have willingly entered into a covenant of love and I am married to Him in spirit, mind, heart and soul. It's His house I prefer. Even while I dwell on the earth my heart demands a place close to Him. For now I have purposed in my heart to teach others as the Lord's love has taught me to follow the "<u>Cardinal Rules to Ride</u>," and to remain close to the Father's heart. Each day I will mount my white horse and ride high where my heart deserves to be with the ones I love, preferring a love unified, living in the life of love, blessed by the will and purposes of love, enabled by love. I ride bearing and delivering the fruit of love to the earth the fruit; purpose and destiny that brings fourth truth and cuts the prisoners free. I bring the truth of love. I present the indisputable evidence of love. I am the alabaster jar of ointment poured out for all to see. I am the White Rider.

To appoint unto them that mourn in Zion, to give unto them beauty for ashes, the oil of joy for mourning, the garment of praise for the spirit of heaviness; that they might be called trees of righteousness, the planting of the LORD, that he might be glorified. (Isaiah 61:3)

My pen belongs to the Lord God. My will is from the Lord God. My heart belongs to heaven; my breath comes from the atmosphere of heaven. I am held by heaven today in the power of the Holy Spirit to prophetically announce I am betrothed unto Jesus in the beauty of holiness to proclaim the reign of righteousness.

The reign of righteousness is for those who ride unto love; for this I stand in allegiance to heaven, my heart captured by love, my spirit at one with love, and belted with truth. I must write and say that the <u>Cardinal Rules of Riders</u> from Jesus are now and have become my way of life.

I am sending out an invitation for all those who would like to join us at the tabernacle at the table of the Lord. It is in the company of His goodness and holiness as our reward and portion as the White Riders. So today, in the company of angels I'm sending out a signal with the pages of this book as a flare shot into the sky.

To the White Riders, I say, "There is a place for your hooves to be heard. There is a tabernacle table prepared for you to commune with Him and His family. This sound is to be heard around the earth, for those who will choose to live, not according to the world, but to breathe the breath of God. I believe He is inviting those who would prefer to dwell with Him above all dwelling places to come and dine with Him at His tabernacle table and enjoy the benefits of the King of Kings and the Lord of Lords."

To the assembly of those who live unto love I say, "Die unto the world. The Father is waiting to dine with the White Rider's of the earth who realize the worth of the return of heaven and who choose to live as a piece of heaven on the earth. To those who realize the potential that one life may bring that is lived unto the heart of God. To those who desire to feast on His words and who choose to live unto the five <u>Cardinal Rules of the Riders</u> that the heavens have now released instruction."

This is the message from the way, the truth, and the life of the true and first risen White Rider to the White Riders of the earth.

Chapter 16

Commencement

"I have prepared a place for those who love Me with all their heart, all their strength and all their soul. A place reserved for those who have captured the Father's heart, who know that our love is important in every way, and is worthy of a place to thrive. Without the intimacy of the Father, Son and Holy Spirit in the high places of holiness, love would have no place to grow. Love is worthy of a place in holiness, a place above the storms, trials and tribulations of man," says the Lord.

"There is beauty in holiness, true beauty. The world's view of beauty is vanity.

The world's treasure is in money. But I see beauty in those who ride high next to My heart. I've seen beauty and beauty only exist in holiness. My children are beautiful to Me. I call them My own. Greed separates the hearts of My children from Me and separates family on the earth. I am a merciful God. I give to those who lack. Lack would be unknown on the earth if not for the hands of greed and vanity. It can be found behind the disintegration of the family. I am a merciful God. Allow Me to reveal true beauty. Beauty belongs to Me. Beauty is My design; I am the author and finisher of it. I am a merciful God but the grave has no mercy," says the Lord.

"I am calling White Riders once again from the earth. My Son and I are training them. I'm teaching them to ride against vanity. I'm teaching them to ride against greed. I'm teaching them to go underneath enemy lines of greed and vanity to reach the lost and impoverished. White Riders ride on behalf of the kingdom. Power and authority are invested in them because they are worthy. They wear an incorruptible crown of holiness. They see as the Father sees, through the glory. They move with the heartbeat of heaven," says the Lord.

"They live to please the Father's will and not their own. I am a God that requires holiness and the beauty of it to attain the incorruptible crown that My Riders wear to signify heaven has invaded the earth. Because I love My children, they represent me as they ride for the love of all My children. There is enough love for all My children of the earth. It's full and it's running over. There is enough, I have supplied enough. I have spoken. My intents and purposes are here. My wisdom is known and enabled," says the Lord.

"White Riders live to know the richness and the beauty of holiness, and they are My life upon the earth. My will be done on earth as it is in heaven," says the Lord.

> *And he shall turn the heart of the fathers to the children, and the heart of the children to their fathers, lest I come and smite the earth with a curse.* (Malachi 4:6 KJV)

Chapter 17

Around the Tabernacle Table

Jesus pulled out my chair inviting me to a large rectangular golden table. This table, where my love for them draws me, is familiar and I know I'm seated in heavenly places. The table is always full of food and drink of all delicious kinds, especially my favorites. As I first approached the tabernacle table the beautiful green meadow around it was empty. I was advised that today's agenda included the angels bringing messages they wanted to deliver. Soon Jesus gave the angels our okay and they seemed to come out from hiding, and we were surrounded. They began to celebrate around the table with dance and song. The angels joined us at the table filling the remaining seats. We held hands, bowed our heads and ask for the Father's will to be done. A familiar angel, one particularly known by my earthly family and I, held a handful of messages she presented for input which I will share in this segment of the book. The messages were read by this angel and the divine interpretation is as follows.

The Message from the Scribe Angels

Love is a song, love is a dance, and love is a celebration of the heart. The heart causes our feet to move. The heart causes all good things to be remembered. Love is cautious with other's hearts. Love is generous and beautiful. It cannot be bought or sold, or captured in a bottle. Love is divine. Love is simple. Love is cherished above all within the heavenly courts. Love is and always will be real. To perceive love is to perceive heaven. To be in love is to have tasted the wonders of it. To sacrifice for love is of the highest honor. To be captured by love is to relinquish one's own rights to be released into more love. We as one are unified in heaven, for love unmistakable. It is for this love we send our message to the earth today (03.18.2011). Let the earth sing for those who hold our love as the highest priority.

The Message from the Youth of Heaven

The small ones of heaven have requested a voice on the earth, this is from them to the small ones of the earth: "The life we now have is good. We live in the middle of heaven and we play loudly. We enjoy living here, it's the best. We laugh and sing and have fun all day. And the Father loves us like no other. We don't cry here because were too happy for that. Everyone from earth is welcomed to join us. We invent new games to play with new people all day long. We want the little ones of the earth to join us to know we love them and we invite them.

There is lots of love here like drinks from the sky. So when the Father says to come to heaven you will know we want you here," says a small one.

The Message from the Four Living Creatures

"On this day, a commencement has begun for we are found in more glory than we have ever known. We are the ones near to the heart of God and we shine from the beauty of His face. We are here to proclaim our power of purity. These are the last days and the glory of the Lord is full in His place of power and authority. We are four but we are one," says the Four Living Creatures.

"We, the four living creatures, are a symbol of purity, power, unity, and love. We are here to bring word and testimony to the unity of love. This is our life; this is our service unto God to live in unity as one and to proclaim the power of unity. Love is the bond and conductor of unity. We are pure because our power comes from love. We are four as one living in unity of love and the power of it. This is our great service and our great honor to be a symbol of the highest honor," says the Four Living Creatures.

"To live amidst one spirit of unity, one not four, is our great power. We proclaim to be as much unified as diversified and to be as one, in unity with the will and service unto God, for this is the true kingdom and the power of it. This is a worthy proclamation," says the Four Living Creatures.

The Message from Risen White Riders in Heaven to the White Riders on the Earth

"We, the former White Riders of the earth, have assembled to convey a message to the current White Riders of the earth: You don't ride alone; you ride in unity of mind, body and spirit. You must listen, take direction, and take orders from the former White Riders. You will need to listen and obey those we have placed in command and that know we all ride for one purpose, one goal of the heart. The earth will say it can't be done. We are a living testament that it can. We ride not unto ourselves but unto the will of God. We live unto the will of God and our blessed by it.

You riders of the earth must *unify in the power of love*. You must *unify in one heart beat of love towards heaven.* The sound of your horses' hooves from heaven's floor pleases the Father and He looses His strength, favor and blessing from heaven. You must *keep your focus and your ears towards heaven* as is your heavenly mandate. Heaven hears and knows your needs. Your needs will be met by the treasures and riches of heaven. Look to heaven and not unto the world for your needs and they will be granted.

This army of the Lord rides high above the infiltration of the world and is supernaturally equipped with power, wonder, grace, mercy and compassion. They will be as salt and light. They will be keen to hear and to be led by the voice of the Father and of the Son. This is the heritage of the servants of the Lord; the faithful followers of the risen Lord."

We bestow honor,
~the former White Riders of the earth.

From the Messenger Angels

"All of heaven bows to the work of the Lord on the earth and that love may carry out its mission and mandates; to receive the lost as the sons and daughters of God in justice, mercy and love," says the Angels.

"Great grace,"

"We thank you."

"A gift of love is the greatest gift anyone can receive, ride high," says the Messenger Angels.

Chapter 18

A God of Beginnings and Not Ends

The Holy Spirit and I moved from the throne room down the portal to earth, into the former prophetic vision. We came to a familiar home, previously visited after the *Battle of Souls*. An angel had brought a former freed captive of the dark warrior's bundles here. We now find him rested from a night of peaceful sleep as a new day dawns as sun shining through a small window.

We watched as he awoke and went to his knees praying with gratitude, "Father, Your kingdom come, Your will be done on earth as it is in heaven unto me."

He remembered the promise of the faithful Father during their throne room encounter after his freedom was purchased by the End Time Army.

"I will make you a promise that if you follow Me and remain in Me you will continue to receive life and will live with Me forever. Beloved, remain in Me and I will see to it that your darkness is turned into light. As you remain in Me you will become as light just as I am and suffer darkness no more. I send you with My blessing, My child. Be of good cheer for I have overcome the world."

A light portal appeared as his prayers are carried to heaven as a gift of his heart to the Father's feet. The Father picks up the gift and with His scepter sends angels to soften his heart with the love of God and glory. Grabbing his Bible, the former captive sets his path towards church. Once inside the church doors he's welcomed and heaven releases a prophetic message that is whispered in his ears during his praise. It was heard and a confirmation sign followed as the light of God shining on his face. As he looks towards heaven now surrounded by an earthly family of God, he presses in to hear the voice of his Father.

A God Rich in Mercy

The Lord spoke to him through the light and glory, "I have plans for you, new beginnings are unending in Me, My son. I've made you in My image for My purposes. I received the gift of your heart as you opened your heart for Mine. My plans are to mold you and make you into My design, to reveal your true identity and to restore the beauty of your spirit that has been lost to the world. I am a merciful God. My plans include you; I'm on your side. I will give you back what the world has stolen from you and what the enemy has taken from you. I remember when I called you forth into existence as a being and I am committed to raising you, My child, to reflect the light and love of where you came from. I'm giving the beauty and the joy and the identity back to you as you seek My face. Guard what is within you as a precious gift, as a treasure. I'm restoring your beauty, your beauty of the holiness of love. It's the true heartbeat of heaven," says the Father.

"We are committed to you, My child, to appoint you into a holy family that cares for you, your needs, and to raise you to spiritual maturity. You are as a city on a hill, a city that is not forsaken. You are Mine and I love you like no other. Like no other before you nor no other after you. Be consistent to choose life and love over the world and the things of the world, as the two conflict and never shall meet," says the Father.

"Let a new harmony come within your heart. Let your heart embrace the sound of heaven again and let the breath of My Son Jesus be the breath of life in your atmosphere again. If you seek Me with your whole heart, a heart unadulterated by the world, you will find Me. I've turned your heart back to Me today with the love of family in the unity of love. I have robed you with the garment of My love. Hear My words and adhere to them for they are life and redemption. Keep your eyes on Me, for behold, I will come quickly into a tousled world of torment and bring order and peace," says the Father.

"You are now adorned in My love and graced with My mercy. I have spoken this to you, My child," says the Father.

Faith in the Unseen

The former captive kneels with his hands on his heart with the light of God on his face. The words of God make a melody within his heart which he had forgotten until love awakened it. Then rising to his feet, he finds his church family on each arm as strength, encouragement and love. He lingers in the foyer of the church, treasuring in his heart the melody now within. He reflects on the Lord's engaging words as he finishes his coffee. As he looks towards heaven, he anticipates the next time he will meet with and hear the voice of his Father; sweet as rain to his thirsty soul.

"Thank you, faithful Lord," he says, smiling as he remembers the Father's promises shortly after his freedom from captivity during his heavenly encounter with his Father.

Exiting through the church doors, a hand reaches towards him, "It was nice having you today."

He leaves, blessed, encouraged, strengthened and loved by the warm embrace of God and God's family. An angel follows him out the church doors; he's not alone. The angel moves before him, pulling up the thorns and planting fir instead.

"Instead of the briar, the angel plants the myrtle tree unto the Father's name, an eternal sign that cannot be cut off, these things he does sight unseen." (Isaiah 55:13 KJV)

An angel goes before him to the place where he dwells, his home. Other angels are already there changing the surroundings. The walls that were dark and dull are now gold and bright with glory. They surveyed his financial position, pushing debt back and releasing good spiritual gifts, good seeds, undetected. Seeing the future, the angels are charged to protect it, and he's helped and encouraged to make decisions to safeguard all that concerns him.

A wind of God is brought by the angels to surround, strengthen and protect him. He is led to a place of peace; an atmosphere that lends itself to commune with his Father. By outward appearances, one might say and even he could question that his life hadn't changed much. But he knew the Father was answering his prayers and keeping His promises. He rests in the peace and sanctity of God.

He lays down in perfect peace as his mind is stayed on the Lord. Holding his hands over his heart and trusting the treasure of the love of God that has been planted there, he dwells in perfect peace. as he anchors his life in the pure light.

"Those who find My mercy find Me and a new day is always upon them like pure light," says the Father.

Chapter 19

The Sun Rose Fierce

The Holy Spirit and I are sent to observe in the enemy's kingdom today. We are undetected as we position ourselves in the office of the Grand Master's counselor. The message on his monitor appeared like a breaking news report of war. "RED ALERT RED ALERT RED ALERT" was the banner that ran across the screen.

The message that followed the alert I perceived to be the following:

The warriors have come back empty handed! The horse's necks are broken by the cheating tactics of the enemy. We have been robbed! In all four corners of the earth reports have come in. They have stolen our bounty and robbed us of our victory. We must retaliate and take back what rightfully belongs to us, by order of the Grand Master.

They have plundered our territory by taking new ground of light; territory that once belonged to the Grand Master's army. Therefore, upon this day we proclaim that "vengeance is in our hands!"

We will call fourth a greater alliance with the world and the servants of it. Know this light army: You have brought hail and brimstone upon you this day, for we have not lost but our anger has been aroused. For darkness will usher in a new dimension of its power. We will establish "new rules" that you and the children of light will abide in! These rules will be of my making. I will rule the world with my rules and give power to my followers in abundance. All those found in the light will be my captives. They will be called trespassers and accused of high treason. The highest punishment will be carried out on those found in the light.

My plans are to rule the earth. I will rise in a power and authority such as the world has never seen before. We have not lost this battle, it has been forfeited due to the actions of cheats, robbers and liars! They have no control over the darkness but have impacted it moving me to unleash greater devices to retain my reign.

I am the god of darkness and the earth belongs to me! The dwellers of the earth have forfeited their rights and life to me! I pronounce today the battle continues. I am bestowing more power and authority on my servants and followers than ever before.

This is the day we awake to the "new rules" of the Grand Master. The tempest will occur; the night will be darker than dark, the punishment higher than high, and the power granted more significant.

We will overtake what has been stolen from us and declare victory against the thieves. The dark horses are a small price to pay to unleash the fury of the Grand Master.

~Grand Master
Signet Seal

Chapter 20

The Sealed Scroll

The sealed scroll with the Red Alert message inside it is sent down to the earth via a dark horse from the Grand Master's kingdom. The dark rider delivers the scroll to the dark commander who has been keeping watch in the high, black fort.

Handing it to the dark commander, the dark rider exclaims, "See these orders are carried out!"

The commander immediately turns to a high tech computer system and inputs the message which is seen as red laser lights running in lines against a dark night sky, going forth into the world dark force of satanic worshipers.

"It is done!" exclaims the commander of the dark army.

Once again a dark army assembles and stands before the commander within the high fort. The earth's witches and warlocks appear first riding wolves. Behind them are the dark riders. They move out as if looking to discern where the light is coming from and head toward a familiar house. It is the home of the young man recently released from captivity during the *Battle of Souls*. His house had been cleaned and gleams of gold from the transformation work of the angels.

There is a path leading from the promised one's house to church. Its light attracts the attention of the dark army. They don't stop at the former captive's house but follow the path of light. First the wolves and then the dark horses and riders with their hooves pounding move along the path of light leading to the church.

They soon approached the church. The dark army was so large the church grounds could not contain them as they settled around their new assignment. The warlocks and witches approached the doors of the church. Their garments of purple with black hooded robes concealed their true human features. They were each wearing crucifixes on long neck chains.

One of the warlocks moved from his wolf and held his crucifix up as protection as he walked through the church doors. Feeling noticed at times he flashes the crucifix on each side of him until he finds a forward seat. Soon he's joined by a few other wolf riders who choose seats directly behind

C. L. Thomas

him. The crucifixes they wear have been dipped in the blood of the innocent, leaving a dried bloody appearance on their fingers as they cling to them for spiritual "well being" in the opposing atmosphere.

The covenant hearts of the witches and warlocks are hard and cold towards the worship. They judge those in attendance with vanity, as they are robed in the world's finest apparel to conceal their identities from the true worshipers of God. They mock the worshipers and invite others around them to join in. They quote scriptures and biblical laws in order to contradict any move of the Holy Spirit; even to quenching the Holy Spirit's fire within the atmosphere of the gathering.

Slaves on Horseback, Princes on Foot

The Holy Spirit reveals to me the enemy's strategy in sending his servants into the church. They befriend those in high positions and use worldly rules, church regulations and stipulations to quench those moving in God's power and authority present in the church body. They move as respected, valued pieces of the body, but they are wolves in sheep's clothing. The prominent positions they take within the church body and open the doors to more demonic infiltration, including witches and warlocks. They successfully cohabitate within the body of believers, remaining undetected as they gradually increase in number and strategically push out the light. Their knowledge of God comes from their heads, and they use legalism as their bible. They are granted the world's power from their master just above and flatter with words of vanity. They are rich with worldly goods as supplied by their evil master.

They form large groups of those with religious head knowledge to control and manipulate. Their strategy is to divide and conquer from within. They move through the church body with the knowledge of the truth but deny its power. The fruit of the Holy Spirit is consciously regulated by those given authority. They implement what they call rules of orderly conduct, which in truth open the door to witchcraft through control, manipulation, vanity, power, authority, judgment, mockery and false accusation. It is as cancer in the church body.

The anointed are moved under foot, pushed aside for these dark ones as they replicate the church body. The spirits the dark ones carry begin to whisper in the ears of those in leadership, speaking counterfeits of the truth. They distract them by urging them to write books of vain babblings to assure even more are swayed off their course.

Chapter 21

Pale Mercy

Within the church sanctuary, the Holy Spirit and I view the enemy tactics. This day the witches and warlocks, dressed in their dark hoods, form a single line sitting on each side of the sanctuary from front to back. Three of the dark hoods sit directly in the center to observe and see to it that their master's orders are carried out within these two rows. They are seated strategically next to the opposite sex; choosing unmarried, trusting, church goers. One by one the witches and warlocks take their black cloaks and cover their target's opposite shoulder as a sign of a covenant unto themselves. Due to a lack of benevolence within the church, they become easy prey and enter into dark covenant vows with the dark ones. Wolves that have lost their riders due to their assignments of marrying within the church body are now running as a pack encircling the boundaries of the church grounds.

"Quicken the dark horses hooves," the orders come from the Grand Master to his earthly commander.

The dark riders advance to the church doors and stand ready, waiting. Soon, a warlock or witch brings a newly bound bride or groom to the dark rider. The one now bound in spiritual chains of darkness is brought to the Grand Master for judgment. He is either converted to dark service or dropped into the large fishermen's nets surrounding each nation. Removed from the mercy the world has to offer, the dark riders act as chariots awaiting the newest captive that has joined his or her heart to a witch or warlock. They are taken on horseback to judgment in the second heaven, where mercy is palest; just above and just below the earth. Banished, they are removed far from creation and the glimmers of natural light.

The dark riders have left the children of the newly bound parent behind, separating them as the dark covenant takes the high place in their parents' hearts. The children are left for the church or the state to care for as they wait for what once belonged to them; a parent's love.

The Trouble Maker

I see one of the children that watched his parent ride away with a dark rider seated in a Sunday School classroom, The child has been deprived of love since the union of his parent to the dark one and his heart is hurting, breaking within. The child's now seen raising his hand in the Sunday school classroom, wanting an answer to the pain within. He is like a baby crying out for milk to drink. The reality of the union of his parent with the dark robed one is setting in as spirit deprivation in the child.

The Sunday school teacher is eager to give the biblical lesson and sees this child's hand raised as interference, even as rebellion.

The child's heart breaks as the teacher exclaims, "You're not listening! Please move away from the other children so they can learn their Bible lesson today."

The child is separated from the other children but still raises his hand as one final cry for help. The teacher glares at the child and labels him a "trouble maker."

The parents form a line just outside the classroom door. The "trouble maker child" is met with a dark shadow of a parent and ushered out the doors of the church. Cold in spirit and hopeless in heart, the child looks into the eyes of another child's parent and sees a glimmer of the light of love he once knew but now is gone. He does not understand what has happened and finds no answer except to take the cause of the lost love upon himself. The dark shadowed parent and the guilt ridden child are met at the doors of the church by a dark rider who pulls them onto the black horse and carries them away on their last ride from church.

The church exit capture progression is repeated by other dark horse riders. Once a parent and child are pulled up onto a dark horse, they quickly leave the church parking lot like a thief fleeing the scene of a crime. Other dark riders try to capture more victims among the progression of cars filled with families leave the parking lot on their way to a family meal. Most were enlightened by the feast of the biblical word that had been ministered to them in the duration of the morning and left untouched by the dark riders.

The dark riders bring the new captives to the second heaven, to the Grand Master's kingdom. A warlock stands before the Grand Master waiting for the dark riders to bring the captives before the Grand Master.

"So this is your new family?" the Grand Master asks the warlock.

"Your orders have been carried out my Lord," answers the warlock.

"Is this one compliable?" questions the Grand Master.

"So far very compliable," replies the warlock. "She asks for the truth."

"The truth she shall get! Take the bastard child to the nets," commands the Grand Master.

Two demons take the child to a dark portal that leads to nets that cover and then drops and hang just below the land on the earth.

"Take her and see that she complies. If she gives you any resistance, bring her back to me," says the Grand Master.

"Yes, my Lord," answers the warlock as he grabs her arm and leads her to "their" house. Inside the house, the child has been placed in a dark, cold room as a prisoner. The parent is bound in servant hood to the warlock. She and her child are now prisoners in her home, kept out of touch with the light and with love. They are lorded over by darkness. The child remembers his prayers but the roof of the house is covered by darkness.

Chapter 22

Love Would Be Nurtured and Live

At the end of the portal from the throne room today was filled with angels and the Holy Spirit revealed a tall light bearing tree that reached from floor to ceiling inside the church sanctuary. Its roots were to stabilize its stature instead of to draw nourishment. The tree had a face of a person at the top and it had strong branches that seemed to stretch into space. The angels came down the portal dancing and twirling with joy and delight, bringing gifts of love to water and nourish this very large tree. Pouring the love they carried from the Father over the head of the tree, its heart beats with eternal life. The angels come and comfortably sit in its branches, as if a piece of heaven dwelt on the earth.

The tree will bear fruit from the nourishment delivered from heaven. Before the fruit is ripe, the angels send runners to the nations of the fruit ripening. As soon as the fruit is ripe, the angels sitting on the branches pick the fruit and take it to the four corners of the earth; the fruit of the nations.

In worship the tree's branches reached high into heaven from the church sanctuary. It lives unto the love and the breath of God. It is able to reach and pull heaven down with its branches. The breath of God swirls around the human faced tree and the wind brings the resurrected life of Jesus, His spirit, upon the tree. Jesus' white horse moves underneath the combined spirit of the tall tree and Himself. The horse begins to climb golden stairs with fruit for the nations and gold from the angels up to the top of the portal and into the third heaven. Easily assessable to the voice of God; they ride above the earth, easily hearing the Father's voice as to where the fruit of the nations needs to be delivered.

Finishing their mandate, Jesus unified with the tall tree's spirit in the form of a warrior dismounts from the white horse, just at heaven's door. A Tabernacle Table awaits them, set for a king. Seeking strength and council at the Tabernacle Table, the tall tree is seated with Jesus. They began feasting on love, breathing in life, and bearing the fruit of life; fulfilling the Father's will, speaking the Father's words in harmony with the host of heaven.

The tall tree acts as a pillar in the church sanctuary. It's outgrown its position and is now bowed beneath a very high church ceiling. Its fruit is full and ripe, and the angels begin to gather the precious crop by the basketfuls. They carry it up the portal into the third heavens. The Holy Spirit and I follow the angels with the fruit, up the portal to find a White Rider wearing a thick armor, robed in white and bearing a unified sword of the prophets. The angels fill both sides of his saddlebags with fruit.

Chapter 23

The Hope of the Nations

The White Rider rides high above the earth from the third heaven releasing the mature fruit of the nations as mandated by heaven, down through the portals of light to the earth. The White Rider rides a white horse, bearing his sword before Him, high above the nets of deception. The fruit is delivered to the four corners of the earth. Once the fruit reaches the earth I see someone, within the boundaries of the light portal, pick it up and eat it. He then quickly moves up the portal into the third heaven to the encounter the one true God. He sits on his Father's lap after eating the fruit. The Holy Spirit and I bend an ear to the intimate conversation that the fruit has enabled between the Father and His child.

At the Mercy Seat

The Father speaks saying, "I am a generous Lord. I give to those who ask of Me. The precious fruit of the earth has been delivered to you today in the name of My Son, Jesus. I am here to speak life to your heart. I'm here to water the seeds of the fruit you have received and to give life to good things implanted in your spirit long ago. I have blessed you today with the fruit of living love that it would be well with your soul. That you would know that I exist, that My love for you lives and we haven't forgotten that you need the spiritual nourishment of love. Find your strength in this love, to live. Love will lead you and help you find your way home again," says his Father.

Then the Father kisses him on the head as he leaves His lap and moves back down the light portal towards earth. Once on the earth again he is fully nourished in spirit. Many gather to hear him preaching of the divine encounter. I see the spirit of his Father descend as he testifies of the Father's great love. Many are saved and set free as he shares a message of his fresh encounter with God, his heavenly Father.

Fruit Bearing Fruit

As the one who has encountered the Lord through the fruit of the nations gives himself to the Lord's presence, he touches all those spiritually hungry who have gathered to hear the truth that is being delivered. Within his eyes the spirit of the Lord shines of love and the crowd is touched by the loving power of the Lord as he ministers a piece of his Father's heart.

It begins to rain living water on all those who are receiving the presence of the Lord through the spirit of the one that has eaten the fruit of the nations. They are cleansed and revived as the rain from heaven falls and the light of the Lord's presence shines on them. The joy of the Lord is on the one who testifies as he lifts his hands to praise. Hope has been delivered, the hope of the nations. The rain of God's loving presence abides and dwells with their souls. It is the hope of the nations, through the fruit of the nations.

I could see the one who had eaten the fruit of the nations and experienced the Father's love begin to pray over those who had gathered to hear his testimony of the divine encounter of love that he had with his Father. As he touches their hands to pray, the anointing he now carries from the fruit of the nations. The Holy Spirit and the White Rider unite within his spirit to release the fruit bearing life impartation over them.

The White Rider carries the blessing of the prophets, and of the God willed saints who have ridden before him. The anointing was that of: *to smell the fragrance of love*. This anointing opens a light portal to all those receiving the united prayer, releasing their spirits to rise and sit face-to-face with their Father; close enough to smell the fragrance of His love.

As they receive the prophecy from the Father, He anoints their foreheads as a sign of blessing to receive the prophet's reward; to smell the fragrance of His love. They leave the portal from the throne room walking in a new way and entering a new day unto the breath of God. They have experienced the breath of life, the breath of love in freedom, and are overshadowed by His glory and light. It's the opposite direction of the world's way spinning towards the pull of love instead of the pull of gravity. Now anointed to see, they clearly discern the nets below the earth and choose the opposite way of life instead. They are freed from the net of deception that covers the nations.

Chapter 24

To Touch the Hearts of Mankind

I saw a thin, dark skinned man in a remote corner of the earth. He was scarcely dressed and knelt beside a river, trying to get a fire started with two sticks.

I then saw a dark skinned woman running from the place where the presence of God had fallen through the one who had eaten the fruit of the nations delivered by the White Rider. The manifest presence of God had changed her spiritual conditions showing her the truth, the way and the life available through the love of the Father. She ran toward the thin man at the river robed in the love of God. A stream of light from the gathering followed her like a sun beam; the gathering of the fruit of the nations had brought forth the fruit of souls. In her excitement, she had run to find him.

As she gave her testimony of how Father God loved her, the thin man could feel God's love come over him as a garment. She spoke of the prayer she had received from the man at the light gathering who had experienced the Father's face. She told of how she had surrendered to the anointed prayers of power and also encountered His face and His words of life.

"He really does love us," she exclaimed with joy and happiness.

"But we have no food," says the man who was dependent on the world and all it would allow him.

The woman reached for his hands with the love of Father God in her heart and with a faith in His love that she has never known before, she prayed to her Father in heaven. Heaven heard her prayer of faith.

Soon, after the prayer of faith the fire was large and I could see the thin man again, in a normal size body dressed neatly and with a hope in God. They lived now unto the Father's love they had new faith in. Protected in the love of God, the angels made sure the river flowed with fish. They laid down in the peace now resting in the love of the Father, secure in His divine care.

Chapter 25

His Own Purposes

We came upon a small golden castle that could only be seen from the eyes of the heart. It's the dwelling place of the woman who had received the impartation of the fruit of the nations and brought it home. The home was in a remote place on the earth. Inside, was the woman who had run home with new hope to the renewed man dwelling by the river bank. She could be found inside this small golden mansion sitting beside a fireplace teaching her children of the love of the Father in heaven. The man of the house is now sitting on a gold throne with the light of God overhead. The atmosphere they now breathe is fit for a king. Their earthly dwelling is heaven on earth. They live unto God and the light of God is on the throne of their new lives.

The angels wash the walls of their new dwelling place with gold for the spirit of life. The angels also transformed their earthly dwelling into a heavenly one as they choose to live unto the breath of God.

The children are protected by the spirit of God. The woman who brought the impartation of the Father's face dwells with her family in the unity of love. They live sanctified in the holiness of heaven. The woman often speaks to her children about God's love as they sit beside the fireplace.

"My spirit was lifted up a light portal all the way to the top where I could see God on a throne in brilliant colors of white," she tells the children. "God the Father motioned for me to come near with a hand of love like He knew me and I wasn't afraid. He grabbed my hand and I could feel peace, His eyes smiled with love for me. I felt wanted and loved and I took a seat on his lap. He told me I was His beautiful child and He was glad I had found my way home today. He taught me of His love for me and how He held me in His heart. He told me how He wanted to bless my life because I was His daughter, not of the world but of Him. His place was beautiful. It sparkled and shined with sweet sounds all around. I wondered how long He would let me stay and breathe the sweet air. He put love in my heart that would bring me home again. Love that would keep me from the world and let me see who I am in Him and that where I belong is in His love.

In His eyes is home, for you and for me. Home isn't four walls; home is love."

She began to pray with the children before sending them off to bed, "Father, teach us and show us the way home, that we would live in that love now and forever more. I bless my children with the love of their heavenly Father, may He continue to teach us His love, Amen."

The Indie Tribe

Through the bush in a remote part of the earth I followed the Holy Spirit today in a vision, similar to the landscape of the home that was restored with the fruit of the nations. We crossed creeks to a cleared area in the midst of the bush. There appeared to be a large, dark painted tribal chief sitting beside a burning camp fire. A large crocodile with razor sharp teeth had its tail and body wrapped around the chief's throne like chair. Other scarcely dressed tribal members encircled the campfire awaiting ceremonial commands from their chief, unaware of the spiritual crocodile.

We move behind the throne to another clearing where a ceremony was taking place. There stood a large carved image. It was hollow at the top and its face had a mouth that was hollow. There stood a tribal man. Sacrificed children went into the top of this statue and blood flowed from its mouth. The tribal man caught the fresh blood in a goblet and brought it to his chief for the evening event.

The chief lifted the blood filled goblet to the sky and exclaimed, "To the god of Indie, may he prosper as we prosper."

He takes a drink from the goblet and passes it to the tribal members around the campfire and they each drink from the cup.

"The god of Indie is at war with us," says the chief. "He is appeased by our blood sacrifice, but there is an enemy that has stormed our camp threatening our ceremonies and our rituals. This enemy is detected in the surrounding areas. He offers hope and peace without sacrifice but in the end he will bring destruction to our way of life. This God is rising up against us. He threatens my throne, the generations it represents and the promises it now brings. We must salute to the one god of Indie and declare that this other God is an intruder and not welcome in our neighborhoods and surrounding areas. We must put an end to this intrusion and put forth our power and authority over it, The blood covenants and sacrifices have been our shield and protection for centuries, and we call upon it now for power and authority to prevail for the centuries before us."

"To the god of Indie, may he prosper as we prosper," the chief says as he salutes with his goblet and drinks from it.

The saluted goblets held high gives attention to the smoke rising above the campfire. The smoke from the flames meets a deep dark cloud, darker than the sky, which forms just above the ceremony. The deep dark cloud has two red eyes and a dragon's face appears and forms from the mass of darkness above. It appears as a winged dragon and then moves into the crocodile's body as it is being fed the left over blood from the ceremonial goblet.

God Will Provide

The vision today shifts to what appears to be the flat lands of Africa. There is a beautiful sunset, as a man with a troubled countenance finishes cooking fish over a campfire beside the river. His family, the woman who had partaken of the fruit of the nations and their two small children, are nearby inside a small home; the light of God sustaining them. As the man brings the fish to the dinner table where there is also some bread, the family gathers to eat. The man's countenance has not changed despite his new founded faith in Father God. He takes a few bites of his food and begins to speak over the children's chatter to the woman.

"The tribal leader demands half of the fish and field yielding from this land. He has appointed a time to meet with me tomorrow. I feel the children are threatened," says the man.

"If we give him half of what we have, we will not have enough for ourselves," she says. "The Lord will provide, we must seek the God of love in prayer."

After dinner, the man takes a walk out to the river, and he looks up to Father God. A light shines upon him and the man begins to wait on God.

"You must leave this boyhood place, away from the strength of the tribal members arm. I will direct your path and lead you to a land of safety," Father God answers.

The man begins to question the outcome, "But I have no skills, no trade, all I have is this land."

"You have love and love will sustain you," says God. "Move away from this dark place. My love and the power of it will move you in the direction you need to go, trust in it."

He returns to his home to convey the message to the woman who's praying inside, "We must travel; the God of love has spoken. We are to go south down the river."

They quickly gather what they can carry and walk into the river, leaving no tracks. They walk under the cover of the dark night. The man carries a large stick that he uses to check the murky water in front of them so as not to walk into water covered predators. The mother carries one child on her back while the other walks close behind them.

At dawn they walk out of the water and Father God supplies fish for their breakfast. After covering the campfire they continue to travel down the river. An angel goes before them. Soon, they find shelter with someone who had been at the same gathering as the woman and had tasted the fruit of the nations as well.

In the meantime, two tribal members have gone to the man's house after he missed his appointment with the tribal chief. When they reported the house was empty to the tribal leader, he angrily demanded that the family be found.

"He owes me. I want what belongs to me," he exclaims.

The family was gone and is now abiding under the safety of the shelter of the Lord and His wings. They awake to a new day, where the sky is clear and blue. They are filled with a peace that can only come from being in the presence of God's family. The angel of refuge moved them passed the enemy's jurisdiction and into fellowship with other members of God's family. The life and light of God flowed from heaven above and led them to a land of peace and prosperity where the children played in safety, out of the grasp of the enemy.

The campfire near the river, a distance from the land of peace, was damp and appeared as if it hadn't been used in weeks. The man was at a new campfire just outside a small, white home positioned among God's family, under the Father God's covering. They are now surrounded by a small neighborhood of white houses and eating bread with those who have also tasted the fruit of the nation's impartation. I could see, not too far from the neighborhood, a newly constructed church. It was erected were the woman first received the fruit of the nations impartation. It was where there used to be a large uncovered platform in a grass and dirt field. Now there was a small, white church with a steeple in place of the open platform. A light portal rested on top of the church where angels would bring handfuls of glory to the dwellers inside. I could see someone up at the top of the portal enthroned in the third heavens, sitting on the Fathers lap. It was a church dweller finding their worth in His eyes, hearing the love in His voice, feeling His heart in the warmth of His embrace; smelling the fragrance of His love.

Chapter 26

A Message to the Seekers of Love

"If the words of this book have brought you to this page, you understand our position. I am reigning in a new day in a new way. The new day coming will be like no other. It will be a day that no one has seen before, a day of new dimensions in God and in His abundant power. For the earth has grown dark in deception and I am a God of truth. Truth is the victory over the land. Truth is the conquering power I choose to use in these last days. Truth is the victory over sin and death. I am a God of truth. Without truth cutting through the darkness, there can be no freedom, no light, and no love."

"From where I am enthroned on high, I see the conditions of the nations. The truth of love and all it represents. Truth gives freedom to love. The nations are in peril as a deep darkness covers the earth. I am releasing, My kingdom swords of truth to those who will speak My words; who will stand unafraid. Without the release of the captives from the nets of deception, the love I have for mankind cannot be received or perceived. My swords are coming to the earth in flaming fire. There will be flaming fire in My voice, for I will not be silenced. I am a God that does not lie. All I say I will do, to every last dot. I am a God that rules over the nets of darkness and deception. Truth reveals deception to let the light of love flow. My people have gotten used to receiving the light of love through deception so when they bring Me their hearts, it strengthens the nets of deception they have learned to live by."

"In these last days I have selected those who will bear the swords of truth, who have unified their spirit with holy fire and power. They are unmistakably marked with My signet ring. They bear My heart, My will and live for My breath, My way. They have been hand picked and chosen to ride with My Son. They bear fruit in His name and are worthy White Riders.

"Before you see them, I will send forth My word to proclaim they are coming and will not tarry. Heaven is full of My love that is to be poured out to the earth for the prophesied salvation of many souls as it is written in My Holy word."

"For it is time," says the Lord, "to bring the Prophets and the sword; the sword that has defeated the enemy with the power of a unified spirit, and tongues as flaming arrows of fire. I will blaze a trail with the Conqueror. The seals of the scrolls have been opened; the Conqueror Rides!"

And I saw when the Lamb opened one of the seals, and I heard, as it were the noise of thunder, one of the four beasts saying, Come and see. And I saw, and behold a white horse: and he that sat on him had a bow; and a crown was given unto him: and he went forth conquering, and to conquer. (Revelation 6:1-2)

Chapter 27

The Conqueror Rides

I saw the Worthy White Rider riding a white horse just above the earth. He was wearing a crown, white robe and holding a sword straight up towards heaven. He spoke in flames of fire. As he rode I saw the swords from heaven of the risen prophets become united with his sword. One at a time they unite with his sword, the risen prophets who lived and died for the words of God have joined the White Rider on the front line. He speaks in one voice, but it is the voice of the many risen prophets. He voice is as one flame of fire; yet the voice is of many.

He uses the lifted sword of unity, with the blood of the risen prophets, to cut the nets of darkness and deception as He rides just above the earth. As the nets of deception are cut on the earth, I see the angels follow in the wake of the White Rider and begin to pour living life filled with the love from heaven from large golden bowls. It flows abundantly behind the Worthy White Rider as a river of life on the earth. The children dance in the river, and the tall trees of God's planting grow deep in the river of love bearing much fruit for the nations. Then many spirits began to flow in the river of life and love, submerged and flowing. The Holy Spirit and I walked in the river as the submerged spirits of the earth flow passed our legs. There was joy, peace, life, love and unity in the river.

Jesus, the Holy Spirit and I took a seat on the river bank with our feet still in the river. We watched as the river flowed with souls, flowing higher and higher bringing the mountains lower and lower. It was as an alabaster jar from heaven poured out in the name of the prophets, in the name of the Son.

"Eternity means that love will live forever because that's what it deserves,"

~Jesus

We moved from the river bank in unity on the white horse, all holding one saddle horn up the portal towards home.

Summary

A Throne Room Prophecy

"Love lives and is seen in the eyes; love flowing from the heart of the Father, where true love exists and manifests itself in prophecy. Love's life is given by Him and received by a Holy God that loves them. Love has a way of bringing His children back home to the heart of God. Love is nurtured and lives in heaven, in the place it was born. Love is clearly defined. Love is worthy of reciprocation, but love must be taught. Love can't be discovered. Love exists in heaven and must be consummated in heaven and brought back down to earth. Love is planted in the heart in heaven, watered by the life in heaven where all things that live are spoken into existence by the mighty Maker of the whole earth. This prophecy is a tale of living love, a planting of the Lord that He may be glorified. It's a tale of a love that lives high above the worldly realm next to the loving heart that created it. A revelation that the only way love can live is to remain close to the atmosphere of the One who created it. Even while on the earth, this love must stay true to a heart of love that lives in heaven and is unadulterated. This heavenly love rides on the wings of the risen One who gave Himself for love. It is a love which the world can't offer. It is a love that's dependent on a life of love, kept high above the worldly deceptions, giving it the position it deserves, eternity."

~The God of true Love.

About the Author

A Jesus' blood washed, Holy Spirit filled and Holy Spirit-led Christian, Cora Thomas's ministry is currently based in Yuba City, California. Cora has been ordained a minister by the pastor's prophetic proclamation during a service at Christian Praise Center, Cornelius, Oregon, under the authority of the Holy Spirit. She carries an apostolic, prophetic, healing mantle to love and serve God. In demonstration of that mantle, Cora has moved into a ministry of divine prophetic proclamation and creative miracles, with the anointing to see into heaven.

The following are the Ministries in which she has served:

~ Sunday school teacher, Carlton Assembly of God, Carlton, Oregon

~ Anchor of Salvation ministries, Vancouver, Washington

~ Portland Outpouring, River of Life Ministries, Portland, Oregon

~ Healing Rooms, Vancouver, Washington

~ Humble King Ministries, Clackamas, Oregon

~ Women's Aglow Leadership home group meetings, Vancouver, Washington

~ Women's Aglow Teen, Vancouver, Washington

~ Bethel Church, Healing Rooms, Redding, California

Other Books:

Memoirs: Reflections of the Father's Heart

Revelations Reflecting the Heart of the Father

For further information: www.alliedridersofthetruth.com

Allied Riders of the Truth is the ministry the author is currently representing and can be contacted for prayer group meetings as well as book signings at the web address: alliedridersofthetruth.com. May the light of Gods love follow you as the noon day sun.